KNOTS
AND
R GS

Steve Cooper
Chris Palatsides

CONTENTS

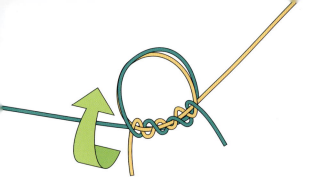

Most anglers employ less than half a dozen knots across the spectrum of their fishing methods. The knots most likely to be used include a Blood knot for tying on a hook; a Snell for a second, fixed hook; a loop knot for lures or flies; a line-joining knot such as a Double Uni; and maybe a Bimini Twist Double, if the angler is into game fishing. Freshwater fly fishers tie a Nail knot to attach a leader-to-fly line while saltwater fly fishers use loop-to-loop connections.

Choosing a knot for a given application is not that hard, so long as you know how to

tie it. There are a wide range of knots available and some have specific uses: the Slim Beauty is designed for joining braid to monofilament, and the Dropper loop knot will suit surf fishers using fixed Paternoster rigs. The aim of this book is to show readers the options available, and explain how to tie a knot or rig to suit.

The knots and rigs described in this book were selected on the basis of covering as many options as possible. Some knots are basic, and in common usage; others suit New-Age lines and techniques.

KNOTS

The golden rule of knot tying is to avoid haste:
take your time, and think about what you are doing.
When a number of knots are used in a rig, and
those knots are tied in haste, then you increase the
chance of knot failure. This is exacerbated when
tying complicated knots that require a higher degree
of concentration.

Knots break when they slip, and knots slip when they
are tied incorrectly. This is often the result of too many
turns, or a failure to pull the knot securely. Putting too
many turns around the standing line is a common
problem. What happens is that the more turns there
are, the harder it is to draw the knot down securely.
On a dry line, a knot that isn't lubricated will resist
being pulled snug. The solution is to lubricate the line
with saliva. When this is done, the line will draw down
more easily, and snug up tight.

Another group of knots which deserve special attention are boating knots. Every weekend thousands of small boats are launched from boat ramps into rivers, lakes, bays and even the ocean. Keen anglers take their boating seriously, however too few give enough thought to the knots they employ. What is the good of finding fish and dropping the anchor only to have a knot on the anchor come undone? Or how about coming in to a mooring jetty after a day on the water and having your knot slip while you are walking up the ramp to collect your car and boat trailer? It happens. So, we have also included some knots that will come in handy on those days when you are using your boat.

Blood knot

The first fishing knot many anglers learn is the Blood knot, used to connect a lure, hook or swivel. The major failing of this knot is human error. Some anglers attempt too many turns around the standing line. The maximum turns this knot needs for lines to 3kg breaking strain is 5; for lines to 7kg breaking strain it is 4; and if you are using a 24kg line then 3 turns will suffice. A problem with the Blood knot comes when you decide to lock it. Pulling the tag end can force the last wrap to 'roll over' the next turn and create a twist or stress point in the knot. The best alternative knot to use is the Uni knot, which is easy to tie and never fails when tied correctly, regardless of line, this includes braid.

1. Pass the tag end of your line through the eye of the hook and back up toward your main line.

TO MAIN LINE

TAG END

2. Create a second loop by passing the tag end back through the eye of the hook. Now complete a series of 5–6 wraps back up and around the main line. The heavier the line being used, the less wraps required.

TO MAIN LINE

TAG END

3. Now bring the tag end back through the 2 loops created earlier near the eye of the hook.

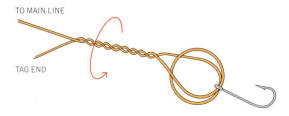

TO MAIN LINE

TAG END

4. You have now created another loop above. Return the tag end back through here and begin to tighten the knot without locking it at this stage.

TO MAIN LINE

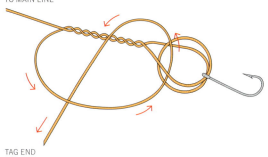

TAG END

5. Lubricate the knot well and gently tighten by applying even pressure and sliding the knot down toward the eye of the hook. Trim the tag end to complete.

TAG END

Cats Paw

The Cats Paw is used as a loop connection to join a double to a swivel, a loop-to-loop connection when fly fishing, and as a fast connection for knife blade lures.

Keep in mind when employing this knot in your terminal system that there are inherent dangers in using a connection where there are 2 strands of line but no actual knot. It is important to have both strands the same length when constructing this connection.

1. Start by pulling the end of the double through the swivel or ring.

2. Fold the end of the double back over itself. This creates another hollow space to work with.

3. Roll the swivel in a circular motion through the central hollow space created. This can be done with 3–6 turns, depending on the thickness of the line used.

4. After lubricating the twisted loop of line created, apply even pressure and slide the knot steadily toward the swivel.

Homer Rhode loop

A popular knot in northern Australia, the Homer Rhode loop is a simple knot, quick to tie and suited to lure or fly. It is a toss of the coin whether you use this knot or the Lefty Kreh loop knot. Both knots are excellent.

1. Start by making an overhand loop in your leader material prior to attaching your lure.

2. Thread the tag end of your leader through the attachment point of your lure.

3. Pass the tag end of your leader back through the overhand knot created earlier. Make sure that your leader enters the overhand knot on the same side it came out.

4. Holding the lure in one hand, and the 2 ends of your leader in the other, pull in opposite directions to tighten the knot.

5. Once tightened, pull on the tag end of your leader to slide the knot toward the lure.

TAG END

6. Create another overhand loop using the tag end of your leader. Be aware that the point at which you tighten this loop will be the size of the final loop.

TAG END

7. Holding the lure in one hand, pull the tag end to make this second knot as tight as possible.

TAG END

8. Pull on the longer leg of your leader to make the first knot slide back up against the second knot, locking them together, forming the loop. Trim the tag end to complete.

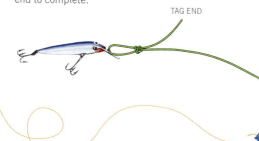

TAG END

Improved Clinch knot

A variation on the Clinch, the Improved Clinch knot is used to attach hooks, swivels and some lures. It won't fail, but to ensure a good knot, lubricate before pulling tight to lock. Like the Clinch, too many turns will spoil the knot. We suggest 5–6 turns for a 3kg line, and 4–5 for a 7kg line. When you are working a 24kg line, 3 turns will suffice.

1. Pass the tag end of your line through the eye of the hook and back up toward your main line.

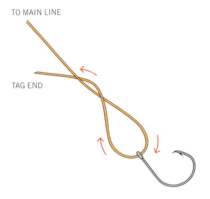

TO MAIN LINE

TAG END

TO MAIN LINE

TAG END

2. Complete 5–6 twists back up the main line. The easiest way to do this is by placing your finger through the bottom loop and twisting in a circular motion. The heavier the line used, the less wraps required.

3. Pass the tag end through the lower loop near the hook, and then back through the new loop created above it.

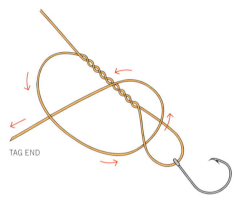

TAG END

4. Lubricate the knot well, then gently tighten the knot and slide it down toward the hook. Trim the tag end to complete.

TAG END

Lefty Kreh loop knot

Lefty Kreh is the world's best known fly-fisher.
There are several variations of Lefty's loop knot but we
have decided the old gentleman deserves the credit.
This loop knot is also useful for attaching lures.

1. Start by tying a normal knot toward
one end of your leader, but do not
fully tighten it.

TAG END

2. Pass the tag end through the fly or
lure you are using, and return the tag
end back through the original
circular loop.

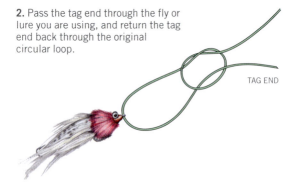

TAG END

3. Start wrapping the tag end up and around the main line. This should be done a minimum of 3–5 times (this will vary depending on the line thickness).

MAIN LINE

TAG END

4. Bend the tag end around and pass it back through the original circular loop. Lubricate the loops and tighten using even pressure.

TAG END

5. Finally, trim the excess off the tag end.

Palomar

A simple knot that requires more line than usual, and for that reason is not popular with fly fishers who see their leader disappear too fast. The Palomar knot has found a niche among soft-plastic fishers tying lures in drop shot fashion, or anglers wanting to rig a hook to a hasty Paternoster and use an extended dropper loop-style leader. The knot does not suit lures with treble hooks, as the lure has to pass through the loop.

1. Double up your line to make a loop. Pass this loop through the eye of the hook.

2. Create an overhand knot using the loop that has been passed through the eye of the hook.

3. Slide the hook back through the original loop. After lubricating the knot, hold the hook in one hand and the double line above the knot in the other hand, and tighten using even pressure.

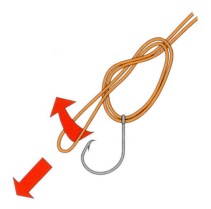

4. Finish the knot by pulling it tight after lubricating the line.

Perfection loop

A strong, effective knot for tying an end loop in heavy monofilament, it is most commonly employed to attach lures and flies. A difficult knot to tie at first, once the technique is mastered it is fail-safe, so follow the instructions to the letter.

1. Start by tying an overhand loop toward the end of the trace you are using. Make sure you leave enough of the tag end hanging out to complete the loop size and knot required.

TAG END

2. Thread the lure through the tag end, returning the tag end through the overhand loop created earlier.

TAG END

3. Now take the tag end back behind the main body of trace, and return it back under and through the overhand loop.

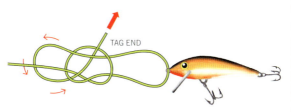

TAG END

4. To tighten the loop, take the tag end and loop in one hand, and the trace in the other. Lubricate the line, and pull both hands in opposite directions. Trim the tag end to complete.

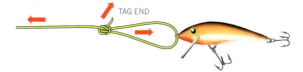

TAG END

Snell

Not as popular as it should be, the Snell is a
100 per cent knot that is best suited to straight hooks
with an upturned or downturned eye. As the Snell
creates a direct pull, it is not recommended for offset
hooks like Suicide patterns.

1. Thread the tag end of your line through the eye of the hook.

MAIN LINE

TAG END

2. Create a loop in the line you passed through the eye of
the hook; make sure you lay the tag end parallel to the
shank of the hook.

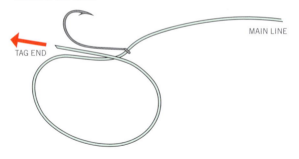

MAIN LINE

TAG END

3. With one hand hold the tag end and top of the loop created tightly against the shank, near the eye of the hook. With your other hand take the end of the loop nearest to the base of the hook and begin winding a series of 6–8 loops around the shank. Make sure that even tension is kept at all times.

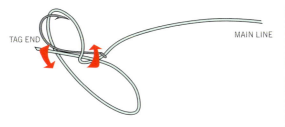

TAG END

MAIN LINE

4. Keep even tension on the wraps created and, after lubricating the line, pull the main-line end to tighten the knot.

TAG END

MAIN LINE

5. Trim the excess line on the tag end to complete the knot.

MAIN LINE

TAG END

Snood

This variation on the Snell is employed when the angler intends fishing more than 1 hook on the leader and wants both hooks fixed. It is in common use for snapper in Victoria and South Australia.

1. Thread approximately 20–25cm of the nylon leader through the eye of the hook. With one hand pinch the nylon leader to the base of the hook and hold firmly. With the other hand hold the longer end of the leader and prepare to fold it back toward the base of the hook.

TO MAIN LINE

NYLON LEADER

TAG END

2. Next, start wrapping this part of the leader down and around the shank of the hook; this can vary anywhere from 4–7 times, depending on the thickness of the leader.

TAG END

3. Now thread the end of the leader you were just wrapping with back up and through the eye of the hook.

TAG END

4. Pull both ends of the leader in opposite directions to tighten and lock down the knot evenly. The final step is to tie your second hook on to the tag end of your leader. For this you can use a knot that you prefer, like a Uni.

TAG END

Thumb Nail knot

This is a fast knot, used for attaching hooks to heavy monofilament. Ensuring the turns of line flow off the thumb in correct order is critical to tying. For this reason, and because the knot suits larger diameter line, 3 turns are recommended. If you do more than 3 turns the knot becomes more difficult. When pulling the knot snug, do it slowly by holding the hook and pulling on the loop against the tag end of the line.

1. Pass the tag end of your line through the eye of the hook or swivel you are using. Return the tag end to create a loop, and lock it between your thumb and forefinger. Leave approximately 10–15cm of the tag end hanging.

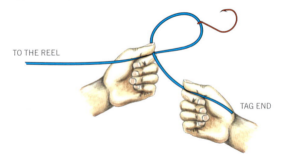

TO THE REEL

TAG END

2. Take the tag end of your line in your other hand and create a series of 3 wraps around your thumb and the loop of line created earlier. Start the wraps from the base of your thumb, working back up toward the top.

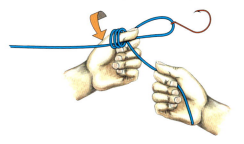

3. Now take the tag end and pass it back under the 3 wraps created earlier around your thumb.

4. Lock the main line and tag end together in one hand and then grip the hook firmly with the other. Now the knot can be formed into shape by pulling your hands in opposite directions. Lubricate well prior to sliding the knot down to the eye of the hook and locking tight. Trim the remaining tag end to complete.

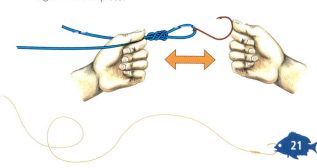

Uni knot

Uni stands for 'universal' and, whether using braid or monofilament, this is a 100 per cent knot that is easy to tie. The key to this knot is to draw it together slowly, rolling the line as you do so, and making certain it locks when drawn up tight.

1. Pass the tag end through the eye of the hook and return it upward.

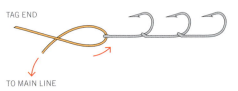

TAG END

TO MAIN LINE

2. Create another loop by running the tag end back toward the eye of the hook.

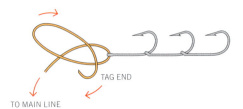

TAG END

TO MAIN LINE

3. Make a series of wraps in an upward direction around the 2 lines that originally passed through the eye of the hook. The thicker the line, the less wraps required.

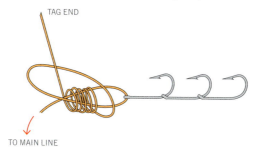

TAG END

TO MAIN LINE

4. Lubricate the knot, and gently pull it tight.

TAG END

TO MAIN LINE

5. Slide the knot down toward the eye of the hook and trim the tag end.

TAG END

TO MAIN LINE

Uni-to-Spool

A simple way to join line to a spool. To avoid slippage and maintain the knot's position to the line wrapped on the spool, draw the knot tight while holding the line on the spool.

1. Double wrap the end of the line around the reel spool.

TO SPOOL
OF LINE

TAG END

TO SPOOL
OF LINE

TAG END

2. Create a loop in the end of the line, facing the tag end away from the spool.

3. Make a series of wraps in and around the 2 lines that are created by the loop and main line running away from the spool. The thicker the line is, the less wraps required. Start with an average of 5–7 wraps.

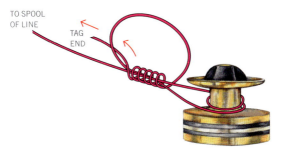

TO SPOOL
OF LINE

TAG
END

MAIN LINE

TAG
END

4. Lubricate the knot, and gently slide it down toward the spool to tighten. Trim the tag end to finish.

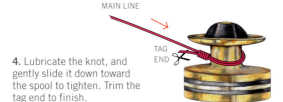

KNOTS ● Terminal connections

Albright

Some of the so-called 'old knots' are still as good as, or better than, the later variations. The Albright knot, which was developed in the 1950s, is a prime example; neat and easy to construct, this is a joining knot that every angler should learn.

During the high-speed spin boom of the late 1960s and 1970s, it was called the Shock Leader knot, and used as a heavy- to light-line connection. Saltwater fly fishers use this knot to join braid to monofilament, or LC 13 shooting heads to braid on saltwater fly outfits. Some light tackle specialists use this knot when joining monofilament leader to braid, although the Slim Beauty knot is preferred by most.

The main problem with an Albright is the potential to slip under extreme load when not locked. To ensure it wont slip, tie a Jim Rizutto finish (Rizutto finish), which is a reverse Uni knot.

The Albright is a reliable connection for:
• monofilament lines of unequal diameter
• monofilament line to braid
• braid or monofilament connection to piano wire.

1. Begin by doubling over the heavier leader. This will create a loop so that your main line can be passed through.

MAIN LINE

HEAVY LEADER

2. Weave the lighter main line down and around the heavier leader approximately 5–6 times.

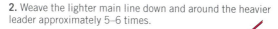
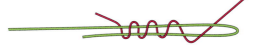

3. Now weave it back up the leader, repeating the same amount of wraps made on the way down. Be certain that the end of your main line passes back through the loop in the heavier leader.

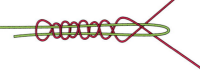

4. Lubricate the lines and start to close the knot using gentle and even pressure. Tighten and secure the knot.

5. Now take the tag end and use a triple hitch (Rizutto finish) to lock the knot so that the tag end can't slip out. Once tightened, trim both tag ends to complete.

Dacron loop

Dacron loops have multiple uses, and make for quick-change connections. Monofilament leaders attached via a Dacron loop are a sensible option for anglers fishing with braid, because the loop connection flows freely through rod guides and leaders can be changed without fuss. This style of monofilament leader-to-braid connection can be used on all tackle from about 7kg through to big game. It is well suited to extended casting situations using baitcaster or threadline reels. Fly fishers use Dacron-loop connections to attach tippets and backing line to a fly line.

1. Start by cutting the length of hollow dacron required, and folding the end over to create the loop.

2. Thread a needle through the middle of the hollow dacron, for approximately 5–7cm. If you are using a needle, start from the bend and work back toward the longer end of the dacron. If you are using a dacron-type crochet tool, you will need to come in from the opposite direction than displayed in the diagram below, so that you can pull the dacron through using the hook. The tool you use comes back to your personal preference.

3. Pass the shorter or tag end of the dacron through the eye of the needle.

4. Pull the needle through the hollow dacron. This takes the dacron back through itself to create the loop required.

PULL NEEDLE IN
THIS DIRECTION

5. Trim the exposed end of the dacron and, by holding the dacron at the base of the loop and the tag end, stretch it apart so that the end pulls back inside and is concealed. At this point you can add a drop of superglue to the base of the loop.

BASE OF LOOP

TAG END

6. Prepare your heavy mono leader by cutting a sharp angle on the end.

MONO
LEADER

7. Trim as much of the dacron ends as possible before inserting the mono leader, to make the whip finishing easier. Introduce the whipping tool, full with thin, nylon-type line.

TRIM FRAYED
ENDS

8. Create a series of wraps working away from the loop and covering the join. When you have completed approximately three quarters of the wraps, introduce a small loop of line, and continue wrapping over the top of it. This 'pull-through' loop will be used to pull the line back under itself to complete the knot.

PULL-THROUGH LOOP

9. Holding the end of the wrapped line, cut off the whipping tool leaving approximately 5cm in length at the end. Pass the end of the thinner nylon line back through the pull-through loop.

PULL-THROUGH LOOP

10. Now, using steady and even pressure, pull out both ends of the pull-through loop. This will pull the end of the line back out under itself.

PULL IN THIS DIRECTION

11. Trim the tag end and seal the top of the bind with a flexible rubber-type adhesive like aqua seal.

The Double Albright is used to join lines of unequal diameters, and is popular among lure aficionados wanting a smooth transition from a monofilament leader to thinner-braid main line. A double is tied in the braid. Some anglers prefer to use a Bimini to make a double, however a Spider hitch serves the same purpose with braid lines of 15kg or less breaking strain. Use the 2 strands as one when joining the thicker-diameter monofilament leader, and remember to melt the tag ends of the braid.

1. Begin by doubling over the nylon leader. This creates a loop so that you can pass your double through.

BRAID DOUBLE

NYLON LEADER

2. Weave the double down and around the nylon leader approximately 6 times.

3. Repeat this the same amount of times, back up the leader to where you started. Pass the looped end of the double back through the nylon leader loop. Lubricate the lines and start to close the knot using gentle and even pressure.

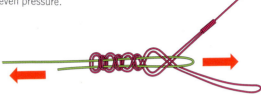

4. Once locked tight, trim the 2 braid tag ends. Using a lighter, melt the nylon tag end and, while it is still hot, roll and flatten this part of the knot using your fingers.

TAG END   TAG END

The Double Blood knot is a popular knot that has stood the test of time. It is used to join monofilament lines of equal diameter, such as when top shotting a reel. This is a neat, 100 per cent knot. A little more complicated to hold during construction than a Double Uni, the Double Blood knot, drawn together and locked, will not let you down.

1. Overlap the 2 ends of the lines you are joining together.

TAG END   TAG END

2. Twist both lines together approximately 8–10 times.

3. Pass both tag ends through the middle opening in the twists created.

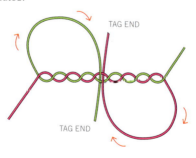

TAG END

TAG END

4. Pass each tag end through the opposite loop created, lubricate and gently begin to tighten the knot.

TAG END

TAG END

5. Trim both tag ends to complete the knot.

The Double Uni is easier to tie than a Double Blood. The Double Uni knot is the one to use when you have the same or unequal diameter monofilament and braid lines. It knots well with dissimilar lines – a copolymer to monofilament for example.

Tying this knot with braid lines is more difficult as braid never seems to want to flow smoothly, even with saliva. So, if tying a Double Uni with braid, pull each knot together, and then pull the knots together slowly, ensuring there are no loose loops.

For mono

1. Lay the 2 pieces of line parallel to each other, keeping both tag ends at opposite ends to each other. Take 1 of the 2 lines and turn it around to create a loop up against the other line.

TAG END

TAG END

2. Now take the tag end of the looped line and pass it around itself and the other line, by twisting it through and around the original loop 4–5 times.

TAG END

TAG END

3. After you have completed the 4–5 wraps, pull up the knot tidily but do not tighten and secure at this stage.

4. For the next part of the knot, repeat the exact same steps already completed, but this time to the other piece of line, now traveling in the opposite direction.

5. Lubricate both lines well and pull the 2 main lines apart from each other to begin tightening both knots and drawing them together.

6. To complete the knot, pull both tag ends tight, and then go back and repeat, pulling both main lines apart to lock and secure the knot.

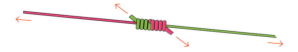

For braid

1. Double the braid line over to form a loop. Lay the mono and the loop of braid line parallel to each other keeping the mono tag end and braid loop at opposite ends to each other.

MONO TAG END

BRAID TAG END

2. Now take the tag end of the mono line and pass it around itself and the braid loop of line by rotating it 5 times through and around the original loop.

MONO TAG END

BRAID TAG END

3. After completing the 5 wraps, pull up the knot tidily but do not tighten at this stage.

BRAID TAG END

MONO
TAG END

4. Repeat the process with the braid loop, but this time wrap the loop around the mono 8 times, working it in the opposite direction.

TAG ENDS

5. After having gently tightened but not locked the knots, lubricate both lines well and pull the mono and braid lines apart from each other. This will draw the 2 knots together.

TAG ENDS

6. To complete the knot, pull both tag ends tight and then go back and repeat, pulling both main lines apart to lock and secure the knot. Finally, trim the tag ends and excess braid loop to tidy it all up.

An unobtrusive connection, the Ducknose's low profile makes it well suited to light-tackle applications. It can take a bit of practice to get right but the effort is worth it as this knot is super smooth through the guides.

1. To start, make sure that both ends of your double are equal in length. Run your thumb and forefinger down and away from the knot that secures your already tied double. This will help you locate the centre and starting point of this knot.

BRAID DOUBLE

2. Pull approximately 15cm of your nylon leader up and through the loop created at the end of your double.

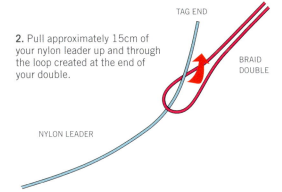

TAG END

BRAID DOUBLE

NYLON LEADER

3. Wrap the nylon leader 6 times up and around both legs of the double. Then bring the tag end back through the loop created between the braid and nylon line. Lubricate both lines well and pull the tag end and nylon leader in the opposite direction to the braid to secure the knot.

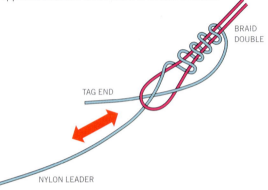

BRAID DOUBLE

TAG END

NYLON LEADER

4. Bend the tag end over and use a lighter to melt the excess tag end away. While the nylon is still hot, roll and flatten the melted line between your thumb and forefinger. This helps secure and flatten the knot.

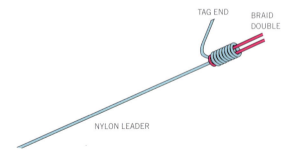

TAG END

BRAID DOUBLE

NYLON LEADER

5. The final knot is flatter and more streamline in profile.

Used to make loops or connections in single strand wire, a Haywire Twist will not let go. Some anglers however, make the mistake of doing more turns than necessary. A small tool can be purchased to make knot construction easier. Those who want a superior, neat finish should pay particular attention to steps 4 and 5. This knot is used for attaching lures, flies or hooks to piano wire when fishing for species including mackerel, wahoo and sharks – anything with razor sharp teeth.

1. Begin by rolling your piece of wire over, creating a neat, even loop. Cross over your 2 ends so that they intersect at approximately a 90° angle.

2. Take a firm grip on the wire at both the intersecting point and the base of the loop. Holding the intersecting point still, twist from the base of the loop in a clockwise motion. Complete 5–6 full, even turns.

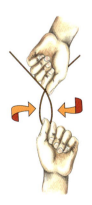

3. Adjust the angle of the 2 ends of wire. Move the longer end upright into a vertical position, and bend the other end down into a horizontal position, maintaining the 90° angle between them. Continue to rotate the horizontal end around and up the vertical end. Again, 5–6 turns will be sufficient. This will create a series of tighter loops.

4. Bend a small section of the horizontal end downward. This creates a lever which will help when completing the knot.

5. With your thumb and forefinger take a firm hold over the twists at the base of the junction. With your other hand swing the horizontal end in a sharp 180° rotation, just skimming past the vertical end, so that you are on the same plane. This will snap off the end piece in a clean neat fashion, and the knot is complete.

180°

The Melville Special is a variation on the Albright. A major difference is that the Melville Special locks off at the rear of the knot, the turns going around the leader line, not the main line. The result is a reliable knot that flows unimpeded through rod guides.

1. Begin by creating a loop in your heavy leader material. Next, pass your braid main line in between the loop, and work it toward the open end.

BRAID MAIN LINE

HEAVY LEADER
(mono / fluorocarbon)

2. Now begin a series of 8–10 wraps, working the braid main line around both ends of the heavy leader material, working back in the direction from where we started.

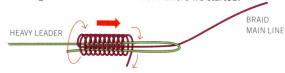

HEAVY LEADER

BRAID MAIN LINE

3. Now create another 4 wraps. This time only going around the 2 lines of the heavy leader and not around the braid main line you are working with. The most critical thing to remember is that all the wraps are made in the same direction and rotation throughout the whole knot.

HEAVY LEADER

BRAID MAIN LINE

4. Now lubricate your lines and apply steady pressure to slide the knots up evenly and lock together. Finally, trim your tag ends, and tidy it all up.

HEAVY LEADER

BRAID MAIN LINE

Mono-to-Braid

A loop-to-loop connection, it offers a quick change for anglers wanting to change leaders. This connection makes joining monofilament to braid neat and easy. Several knots can be employed to create the loops, including a Uni, Bimini Twist or Plait.

1. First slip the monofilament leader loop over the braid loop and line.

MONO LEADER

BRAID LINE

2. Then proceed to pass the end of the mono leader through the loop of the braid line.

3. Continue weaving the mono through and around the braid loop.

4. Lubricate and pull the knot down evenly.

Mono-to-Wire

This system is suited to anglers chasing toothy species like sharks or mackerel, and who do not want to employ a swivel. The terminal end of the main line is snelled to single-strand piano wire. A rectangular loop, turned up at the end in the style of a hook eye, is made in the wire for snelling the leader. To tie wire off, form the loop then make several turns before turning the tag end of the wire at right angles and finishing off with a haywire twist.

1. Start by bending a piece of wire over and kinking the bend up slightly (approximately 45°). Then pass the tag end through the loop and over the outer side of the 2 parallel, straight sections of wire.

PIANO WIRE
TO MAIN LINE
TAG END

2. Now pass the tag end under, around and back over the 2 straight sections of wire.

TO MAIN LINE
TAG END

3. Continue wrapping the line back over itself, working it toward the kinked section.

TO MAIN LINE
TAG END

4. After a minimum of 10 wraps, pass the tag end back through the bend in the wire.

TO MAIN LINE

TAG END

5. Pull the knot tight so that it slides forward and locks itself up against the kink. Then roll the tag end back, creating another loop.

TAG END

TO MAIN LINE

6. Thread the tag end back around the main line in the loop previously created (minimum 5 times). Pull this knot tight and slide it back down, locking it onto the other knot created earlier. Trim the excess line off the tag end to complete.

TAG END

TO MAIN LINE

The critical connection in fly fishing is between the butt section of the tapered leader and the fly line. The knot used to make this connection secure is the Nail knot. Loop-to-loop connections are all the rage in heavier fly-fishing applications, but when you are in the lighter line weights, there is no knot that offers the strength and smooth transition from fly line to butt as does the Nail knot. Tied correctly, this knot will never fail.

1. Lay both your fly line and leader material, parallel to your hollow plastic tube. Leave a longer tag end on the fly leader.

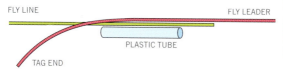

FLY LINE

FLY LEADER

PLASTIC TUBE

TAG END

2. Holding the 3 items snugly together, begin wrapping the longer tag end of the fly leader back over itself, the plastic tube and the fly line. Six wraps will be enough.

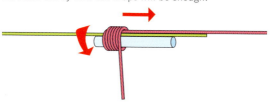

3. Now slide the knot toward the end of the plastic tube, in the direction you were wrapping, then slide the tag end back into the tube.

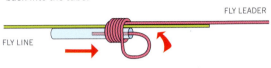

FLY LEADER

FLY LINE

4. Holding both lines and your wraps together, carefully remove the plastic tube. You can now start tightening (but don't lock) your knot by pulling on each end of your fly leader, making sure that your loops sit evenly over your fly line.

FLY LEADER

FLY LINE

5. Finally, adjust and slide your fly line back so that no trimming is required. You can now lock the knot tight and trim the remaining tag end of your leader.

FLY LINE

FLY LEADER

Used to join braid to monofilament, the PR connection is a sure knot but construction is best before going fishing, as it requires a bobbin tool for the whipping and finishing.

1. Begin by passing your braid line through the bobbin, and lock the end of the braid into the side rubber stoppers. Then make a series of 8 wraps around the spool of the bobbin.

BRAID LINE

JIGGING MASTER
BOBBIN TOOL

2. Holding your mono leader firmly between both hands, allow the bobbin tool to hang freely next to it. Now swing it around in a circular motion, like a pendulum, to create 4 gentle wraps around the leader.

BRAID
LINE

MONO
LEADER

3. Once you have done this, turn your hands around to a horizontal position. With your fingers, pinch the braid and mono lines together allowing the bobbin tool to hang freely.

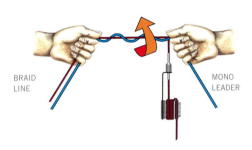

BRAID
LINE

MONO
LEADER

4. Using a circular motion, start spinning the bobbin tool around the heavier mono line. Stop after 4 wraps and pull down on the braid to tighten and level off the knot before continuing. Continue wrapping around the mono, always keeping even and steady tension on how the line comes off the bobbin. After wrapping for about 50mm, the bobbin tool can be cut off. Do not cut the braid off too close to the mono, and allow a reasonable tag length as a number of half hitches are required to complete the knot.

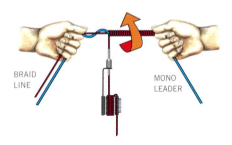

BRAID
LINE

MONO
LEADER

5. Using the end of the braid, complete a series of half hitches around both the main mono and braid legs of line. Tie the half hitches from alternating directions: 1 from above and the next from below. This needs to be done 4–6 times.

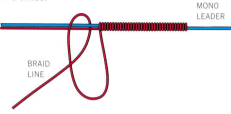

MONO LEADER

BRAID LINE

6. Pull the braid and mono lines apart using maximum tension. This is to help avoid any slippage that may occur later in the knot.

7. Now repeat another series of half hitches just like in step 5. This time wrap the alternating half hitches only around the braid itself, and not around both legs of line. This is to protect the braid from the heavier mono when it is trimmed.

8. To complete the knot, melt the end of the mono and pat it down before it cools. Finally, trim the excess braid, and the knot is complete.

Slim Beauty

A favourite joining knot for heavy to light lines,
the Slim Beauty can be used to join monofilament to
monofilament, or braid to monofilament leader. When
braid is the material used, more turns are required
around the leader line. The value of the Slim Beauty,
apart from its strength, is that it locks down into a low
profile and will pass unimpeded through rod guides.

1. Tie a double overhand knot in the heavy mono leader.

HEAVY MONO
LEADER

2. Gently pull the 2 ends of the leader away from each
other until a figure 8 shape is created.

3. Now feed the thinner-diameter main line through both
loops of the figure 8 shape.

LIGHT MAIN
LINE

4. Wrap the main line around the heavier leader and work away from the knot 7–8 times. Repeat the same amount of turns back toward the knot, and slip the line through the final tag above the knot.

5. Lubricate both lines and tighten the heavier mono first, then tighten the second knot to fit snugly up against the heavier leader. Pull the knot tight and test it, then trim the tag ends.

TAG ENDS

Stopper knot

Tied with a lighter line than the main line, this knot is used as a stopper to control distance between bait and devices such as floats.

1. Begin by laying the thin line up against your main line. It is this thin line that will create the sliding Stopper knot.

MAIN LINE THIN LINE

2. Return the thin line to where you started, to create a large loop.

3. Begin wrapping the thin line around both of the lines together.

TAG END

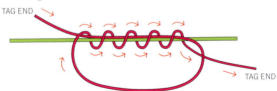

TAG END

4. Once out the other end, lubricate the lines, and pull the ends of the thin line in opposite directions to tighten and finish the knot. Complete the knot by trimming the excess off the tag ends.

Top Shot connection

Braid is best purchased in small doses. The
problem is that it has a smaller diameter than
monofilament and therefore more braid is required
to fill a spool. One way to overcome this is to top shot
your reel, using monofilament as a backing, and
then winding on braid. As well as being thinner than
monofilament for breaking strain, braid material is
harder and can cut a mono line. A Cats Paw does not
need to be locked the way many other knots are, so,
with the combination of double lines connecting, there
is less chance of the braid cutting the backing.

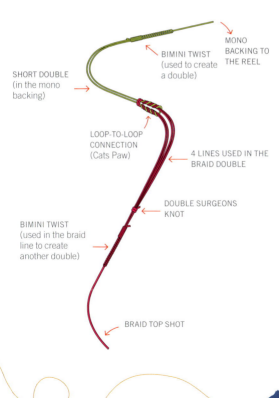

MONO
BACKING TO
THE REEL

BIMINI TWIST
(used to create
a double)

SHORT DOUBLE
(in the mono
backing)

LOOP-TO-LOOP
CONNECTION
(Cats Paw)

4 LINES USED IN THE
BRAID DOUBLE

DOUBLE SURGEONS
KNOT

BIMINI TWIST
(used in the braid
line to create
another double)

BRAID TOP SHOT

KNOTS ◆ Line-to-line connections

Triple Surgeons

Despite the suggestion given by the name, the medical profession does not use this knot. It would be more accurately described as a multiple overhand knot. This knot is great for joining lines but has limitations and should not be employed when one strand of line being joined exceeds 24kg breaking strain: line this heavy cannot be drawn tight enough by hand.

1. Overlap the 2 ends of line that you are joining, by at least 15–20cm.

2. Tie the lines together in an overhand knot.

3. Wrap the ends of the lines back through the large loop created, in opposite directions, 3 times each.

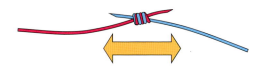

4. Lubricate the knot and apply even pressure while pulling all 4 ends of line tight. Trim the tag ends neatly.

Twisted Leader (Bungie knot)

Fly fishers wanting to make up a tapered leader from a single strand of monofilament use this knot. When rolled tight enough it offers the angler a bungie effect that allows more shock absorption from a high-speed pelagic. In 10kg breaking strain, the Twisted Leader has proven successful on yellowfin, tuna and marlin.

1. After selecting the required length of line (in this case approximately 6.5m), find the middle and move to either side by 1.5m. Fold over in this location and place a hand on each side; this is your starting point. Begin the knot by rotating each hand in opposite directions while simultaneously moving them toward each other.

2. Continue this twisting and moving toward each other until you come to the end of the line. You will be left with a single strand of line. It is at this point, where the 2 twisted lines meet the single, that we need to tie them off. Here we use a Nail knot.

3. Trim any excess line from the Nail knot or leader, and discard.

4. From the knot, measure up approximately half a metre and use this point to fold the remaining twisted line in half. Working from this new location repeat the actions in step 1. You are now twisting the original twist over itself. This gives you the final step in the taper of the leader, a 4-strand twist.

5. When you have completed this section, you will tie a Nail knot just above the end, and trim off the original loop you created at the start. You should have approximately 1m of 4-strand twisted, half a metre of double and 1.5m of single. You can add more strength to this knot by adding a drop of superglue or aqua seal over the Nail knot.

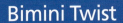

Bimini Twist

Bulky knots are not always strong knots,
however the Bimini Twist is big and strong. It is one
of 3 popular double knots, and the most common
double knot used for lines over 10kg breaking strain.
Dare we say, it is also the most popular double knot
tied by anglers who struggle with the Plaited Double
knot. The real value of the Bimini, apart from its
strength, is that it is easy to construct under difficult
conditions; even when not tied well, it still seems to
hold. The Bimini can be used when creating a double
line to be used: as a leader from a main line to a
swivel, for loop-to-loop connections in fly leaders, or
when you want to join 2 lines of unequal diameter
using a Uni knot. Back tie with a Jim Rizutto finishing
knot, otherwise known as a reverse Uni knot.

1. Begin by doubling over the length of line required for
your double, to create a loop. Place your right hand into the
middle of the loop. Holding both the main line and tag end
in your other hand, begin rotating your right hand in a
circular motion. This will create a series of twists.

MAIN LINE   TAG END

2. Continue this anywhere from 20–30 times
for monofilament line, and 50–70 times for
braid-type lines.

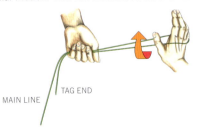

3. This knot ties better under tension, so you will need to place the rod in a rod-holder or ask someone to hold it for you. After completing the number of twists required, look for somewhere suitable to slip the loop over, like a bollard when on a boat. Keeping tension in the line at this point is critical, so when placing the loop over the bollard, make sure to put a working curve in the rod so that there is tension present throughout the main line and the end of the loop. Holding the tag end in your left hand, begin pushing your right finger up through the twists and away from the loop. This will start putting tension in the twists. As it tightens fully, start leading the tag end in your left hand toward your right. You will find that the tag end will jump up on top of the earlier created twists, covering them with another series of wraps over the top.

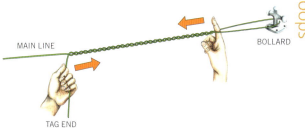

MAIN LINE

BOLLARD

TAG END

4. Continue this action over the top, until all of the twists are covered.

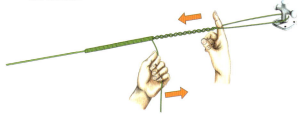

Bimini Twist *(continued)*

5. To secure this together, with one hand grip the junction point where the end of the wraps meet the double. Using your other hand tie a half hitch around one of the legs of the loop.

MAIN LINE

TAG END

6. Take the tag end and create another half hitch around the second leg of the double.

7. Finish locking the knot by using a triple hitch, also known as a Rizutto finish.

8. Now that the knot has been tightened and secured, trim any excess off the tag end.

TAG END

The Dropper loop is a universal connection point used to attach leaders, balloons and soft plastics on a drop shot system. This knot is basic and a must for anglers fishing different techniques from bay and beach to offshore, rivers and lakes.

This knot is well suited to fixed Paternoster rigs and is much better than using a 3-way swivel – a simple device with a penchant for failing under load. There is a design flaw in 3-way swivels in that the extension that leads from the swivel at right angles is in 'sheer' force and can part under a heavy load.

The simple and surest way around this is to tie a twisted Dropper loop. These can be set at any distance above the sinker on the main line. Separate snoods are made up and connected in loop-to-loop fashion. This loop system is best suited for small to medium size species such as tailor, salmon, pinkies and whiting.

1. Create a loop in your main line.

2. Next, overlap the line at the top of the loop to form a smaller loop above.

3. Begin twisting the line of the smaller loop 4 times around and over the larger loop below.

4. Once you have completed the 4 twists, push the middle section of the larger loop up and through the centre of the smaller loop created above.

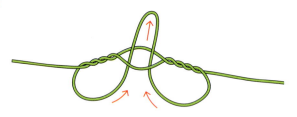

5. Slowly tighten the knot, making sure to lubricate it well before locking it.

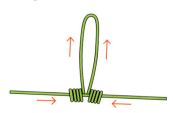

Plaited Double

An alternative knot to the Bimini Twist, the
Plaited Double serves the same function but
advocates claim it is a better knot with more
cushioning effect even though both knots test at
100 per cent. Experienced anglers can tie a 'Plait'
in about the same time as it takes to tie a Bimini. All
it takes is practice. Some anglers will tell you that a
Plait is easier to tie under difficult conditions, such as
fishing offshore.

1. Firstly, you need to measure out double the amount of
line you want your final double to be. Also add on about
another 30cm, this is to allow for the plaited knot. Now
create a large loop with the length of line measured,
looping that extra 30cm of line around and into the middle
of the loop.

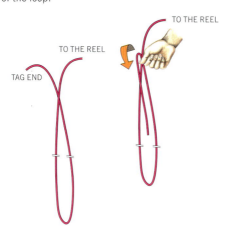

TO THE REEL

TO THE REEL

TAG END

2. Make sure that your line and rod are in a secure position and locked tight. Grip the point where the lines overlap with your thumb and forefinger, this will help with the first few turns and getting the plait started. Try to keep even and steady pressure while tying, as this will give you much better results. You now have 3 pieces of line to plait. Just as you would when plaiting someone's hair, work from the outside into the middle of the other 2 lines; first from the right side and then from the left. Repeat the process until the desired length is reached. The heavier the line, the longer the length; about 8–10cm for a 14kg line.

TO THE REEL

TO THE REEL

3. Now take the shorter of the 3 pieces of line (making sure it is in the middle position) and loop it up back toward the knot you have been plaiting. Make sure you overlap the plait by a couple of centimetres.

4. Now treat the double loop created (which should be located in the middle position) as a single strand and continue tying the plait, working from the outside in. Continue this section of the plait about half the length of the first part plaited.

TO THE REEL

TO THE REEL

5. Pass the long double through the small loop, which again needs to be in the middle position. Then lubricate the plait and, with firm and steady action, pull the tag end tight which will lock the knot in place. Finally, trim the remaining tag end neatly.

Spider hitch

This is the fast method for tying a double leader under duress, such as during a hot bite. Use the Spider hitch on lines less than 9kg breaking strain in monofilament and less than 15kg in braid. Even though the knot is strong and rarely breaks under load, it is not 100 per cent rated.

1. Once you know the length required in your double, create a loop in your line. This is the point where the knot will be formed.

2. Now take the double with your other hand and begin wrapping it around the base of your thumb and the other 2 lines, working it back toward the original loop created.

3. Once you have completed 5–6 wraps, pass the double back through the original loop.

4. Having lubricated the knot, tighten it using equal pressure on both sides.

Anchor hitch

The Anchor hitch is also known as the
Fisherman's hitch and is useful for attaching a line to
an anchor or in most tying applications.

1. Take the end of your rope and make 1 full wrap around
the post.

2. Make a second full wrap around the post without over-
tightening, leaving a gap between the first wrap and
the post.

3. Bring the end of the rope fully
around and under the 2 wraps.
Then push it up through the gap
left between the post and rope.

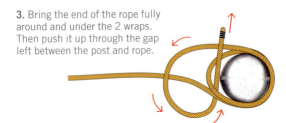

4. Pull the end of the rope in a downward direction to
commence tightening. Now bring the end back around
and under itself, and use a reverse half hitch to lock it
all together.

When you need to create a quick loop in your rope, such as when mooring, this knot is fast and easy to tie, and even easier to undo. Under load, it does not slip or bind. Two bowlines can be linked together to join 2 ropes. Its principal shortcoming is that it cannot be tied, or untied, when under load and should be avoided in load situations, such as on a mooring line that may have to be released under load.

1. You will need to form a loop toward the end of your rope.

2. Return the end of your rope to pass back through the loop created. This creates a larger, second loop or bow shape.

3. Finally, bring the end of the rope back up and through the center of the original small loop. Now apply even and firm pressure to lock the knot tight.

Buntline hitch

This knot traces its origins back to the days of sailing ships and was used to secure the buntlines to the foot of the square sails. Its value was that the knot tended to tighten under the pressure of repeated shaking and jerking by a flapping sail.

1. Take the end of your rope and wrap it around or through the object you are tying to.

2. Now take the end of the rope and make a full turn around the main body or standing end of the rope.

3. Return the end of the rope back up and through the gap that is left beside the rail you are tying to.

4. Complete the knot by passing the rope back under itself, making a half hitch.

Carrick knot

A useful knot when 2 ropes need to be joined.

1. Take the ends of the 2 ropes you are joining together, laying them parallel to each other and rounding the ends inward toward each other.

2. Create an open loop in the lower of the 2 ropes, and then pick this rope up and place it on top of the other rope.

3. Now take the end of the bottom rope, threading it back under the tag end of the rope on top, then back under itself through the middle loop.

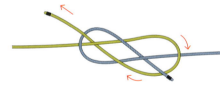

4. Finally, the knot can be locked tight by pulling both ropes with their ends in opposite directions.

Cleat hitch

KNOTS ◆ Boating knots

Used to secure rope to a cleat, this basic knot takes practice to perfect.

1. Begin by wrapping your rope fully around the feet or underside of the cleat.

2. Now take the rope diagonally across the top, and then wrap it back under the point of the cleat.

3. Wrap your rope back over the top and back diagonally toward the opposite end. This will create a figure 8 shape. Now you can use an underhand loop to lock the knot tight.

There are 2 faults with the Clove hitch in that it can slip or bind. It doesn't look secure, but the knot will not let go when tied correctly and can be used to secure fenders. To make the hitch secure, add extra half hitches.

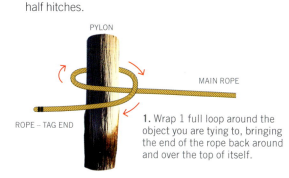

PYLON

MAIN ROPE

ROPE – TAG END

1. Wrap 1 full loop around the object you are tying to, bringing the end of the rope back around and over the top of itself.

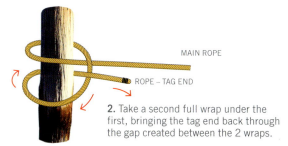

MAIN ROPE

ROPE – TAG END

2. Take a second full wrap under the first, bringing the tag end back through the gap created between the 2 wraps.

ROPE – TAG END

MAIN ROPE

3. Now tighten the slack between the wraps by pulling the tag end and main length of rope in opposite directions.

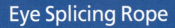

Eye Splicing Rope

Splicing an eye into the end of a rope is better for creating a loop than tying a knot. Loops can be used to attach ropes to anchors or U-bolts, to hold fast on cleats, or even to run a short rope along an anchor rope when you need to bridle the boat against wind or tidal influence.

MELTED ENDS

1. Start by unwinding the end of the rope. Then secure the end of each strand by either melting each end (as in the diagram), or whipping thin twine over them.

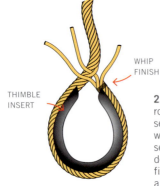

WHIP FINISH

THIMBLE INSERT

2. The thick end of the rope should also be secured at the base, where the unwound sections meet. This can be done using tape or whip finishing over the top with a piece of extra twine. Metal or plastic thimbles can also be inserted prior to weaving (step 3). This helps protect the rope from wearing and abrasion.

3. You may need to untwist the main rope a little to create gaps, making it easier to pass the thinner strands of rope through. You can buy tools to help with this. Using a biro can also help; tape the ends of the rope strands to the end of the biro, and use the front, pointy end like a sewing needle, to guide and push the strands through the gaps.

4. As a basic rule, use 5 tucks or weaves on each strand for general work, and use a minimum of 7 tucks for heavier requirements.

5. Just like any form of weaving, each thin strand is first passed under and then over. This process is continued as you work up the rope. Once complete, melt larger knobs on the end of each of the strands to help lock it all together. Some people run a little tape or whip finish over the top with twine for extra security.

LARGER KNOB TO FINISH

Poachers knot

One of the few knots suitable for use with New-
Age ropes such as Dyneema and Spectra. Bowlines
and other familiar loop knots may not be secure with
these slippery, high modulus ropes and may pull
undone.

1. Take the end of your rope and fold it
over to create a loop. Then wrap it back
under and around the loop created.

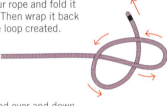

2. Now pull the tag end over and down
to create a small loop at the base of
the larger one that we started with.

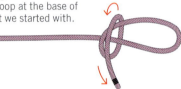

3. Complete this same action to create a
second full loop at the base of the
larger one.

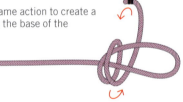

4. Pull the tag end of the rope down reasonably firmly,
this will start to tighten and pick up the slack from the
2 smaller loops. You do not want to over-tighten at this
stage, because you want to leave enough room to tuck the
tag end back through the middle of the 2 small loops and
lock the knot tight.

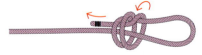

If you have doubts about using a Clove hitch
knot then use this one for the same purpose. It is a
more secure knot.

1. Wrap the end of the thinner rope around the thicker rope
as if tying a half hitch.

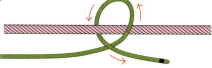

2. Go around and wrap over the first turn again.

3. Bring the tag end back around and wrap it back
under itself.

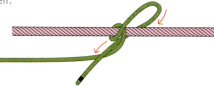

4. Pull the tag end back firmly to pull
up some of the slack in the earlier
created loops.

5. Finish the knot off by bringing
the tag end back around and
locking it tight with a half hitch.

Sheet Bend

This knot is used when 2 lengths of rope of different diameters need to be joined. The thicker rope must be used for the simple loop, as shown. It also works if the ropes are of the same diameter.

1. Take the thicker of the 2 ropes and roll the end over to create a loop.

2. Now pass your second, thinner rope through and over the top of the original loop created by the thicker rope.

3. Now pass the end of the second, thinner rope around the back and down behind the original loop created by the thicker rope.

4. Finally, bring the end of the thin rope back up and under itself, passing it between itself and the thicker rope.

One of the most frequently tied knots, being used in knitting as the first loop when casting on – where it is called a Slip knot – but frequently tied as a noose. It can be used as a temporary Stopper knot, as shown below.

1. Pass the rope through the gap, then form a loop near the end of the rope.

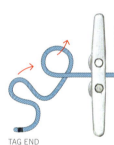

2. After creating the loop, form a bight nearer the tag end of the rope.

TAG END

3. Thread the bight back through the original loop. Finally, pull up the tension to complete and lock the knot. To release the knot quickly, simply pull down on the tag end of the rope. This will not release the knot completely but allow the rope to slide through freely.

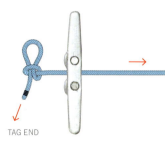

TAG END

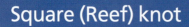

Square (Reef) knot

Intended to be a binding knot and, tied in the right material against a curved surface, the first half knot may bind – but it cannot be trusted. Surgeons use an extra turn in the first half knot – to achieve the binding required while they prepare the second half knot.

1. Take your first rope and roll the end over to create a loop.

2. Pass your second rope through and over the top of the original loop.

3. Now pass the end of the second rope around the back of the original loop.

4. Finally, bring the end of the second rope back around and through the center of the loop. Holding each rope and its end in each hand, pull them away from each other to lock the knot tight.

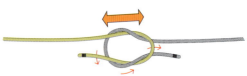

A round turn and two (or more) half hitches are useful for attaching a mooring line to a dock post.

1. Take the end of the rope through the eye or ring you are tying to.

2. Once through, take the end back around and under itself, then thread it back through the loop created, working away from the eye bolt. This creates the first half hitch.

3. Repeat the previous actions in step 2 to create a second half hitch.

4. Apply even and steady pressure, sliding the knot toward the eye bolt to tighten and lock it fast.

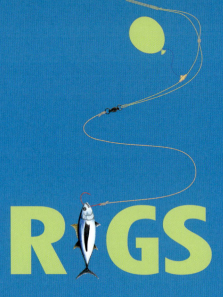

R[]GS

Rigs are the terminal ends of fishing tackle, the critical zone where nothing should be left to chance. Terminal tackle includes leaders, swivels, hooks, sinkers or lures. You cannot be blamed for materials failing, such as swivels, but knots on rigs are another matter.

There are many different rigs promoted in books and magazines and most of these are variations on four simple rigs: Running Sinker, Paternoster, float and unweighted. These rigs can be tailored to suit specific species and the environment the fish inhabit. Take rig recommendations as suggestions, and then adapt them to suit the environment you intend fishing.

Just because a rig is listed under salt water does not mean it cannot be adapted to fresh water, and vice versa. There are no hard and fast rules, fish don't know the difference so be prepared to adapt.

General rigs

A southern angler fishing around Rockhampton
will find a striking similarity in rigs and methods
used. In the Fitzroy River, live prawns are rigged
for barramundi the same way as you would rig a
prawn for bream in East Gippsland. Offshore, over
reef systems, the common rig used is a two-leader
Paternoster, the same as that used by many anglers
bottom bouncing in Bass Strait, Victoria.

In South Australia, snapper anglers favour a Running
Paternoster rig, which is the sinker on a leader that
is free to run along the main line and is positioned
above the leader to the bait. At the southern end of
Port Phillip Bay and in Western Port, this rig is popular
for snapper and King George whiting. It is in common
use where there is current and you want to be able to
feed line out without moving the sinker. Surf anglers
seeking big fish like mulloway or gummy shark use the
same rig. In this case, the leader to the sinker is longer
than the leader to the bait as it is easier to cast.

Wherever you come across anglers fishing with bait,
regardless of location or fish species, the basic rules
of terminal tackle remain the same. And in case you
didn't know, terminal tackle is everything beyond the
rod tip except for the bait and includes hooks, sinkers,
swivels and leaders.

Many books offer a run-down on suggested rigs to use
for different species. Regardless of where you fish,
be it northern or southern Australia, fresh water or
salt water, there are four definitive types of rigs used
when bait fishing. These are Running Sinker, fixed
or Paternoster, float and unweighted. All of these can
feature subtle variations on the same theme.

The thing about terminal tackle is that there are no hard and fast rules, and no guarantee you will catch fish. It is important not to become fixed on rigs just because they are recommended. When deciding on a rig, there is more than simply the fish to consider; factors including terrain and current will have a bearing on the decision-making process.

Even hook sizes and patterns are subjective. There are three basic rules to follow with hooks:

- make sure your hook is sharp
- keep the hook point exposed
- hook size is governed by bait size, not the size of fish you are after.

Anglers can improve their results by adapting and changing to suit conditions. This can be as important as fresh bait. Fishing with unweighted bait is the best system, but has limitations: you can fish unweighted bait in current in relatively shallow water, but you must cast up current and allow time for the bait to sink. The effectiveness of this method depends on the weight and buoyancy of the bait used relative to water flow.

When light bait is used in strong current it will eventually be swept out of the feeding lane and you will have to repeat the process. Baits like prawns and scrubworms work well in current, as the lack of buoyancy allows the bait to sink or hold depth. In any situation where unweighted bait can be used, it should be.

Float fishing is a common method in bays, estuaries, rivers and lakes. Land-based game anglers fishing for tuna and marlin from the rock ledges of southern

New South Wales suspend live bait beneath larger floats, known as bobby corks, or beneath balloons. When you are fishing for big fish, you tend to use big baits so there is no problem keeping the bait down and the way the float sits in the water is irrelevant.

However, if you are after smaller fish, say mullet or trout, then the chances are you would be using a quill float. In this scenario, the float is a bite indicator so its attitude is important. A quill float needs to 'stand' on the vertical plane in the water with just enough of the tip showing to indicate a bite, while the bait is set to remain at the required depth. To get the right float attitude split shot is placed on the line above the bait. It's a matter of trial and error until you get just the right amount of shot to position the float where you want it.

Snapper might be regarded as bottom feeders, but they will take baits higher up in the water column. Most bay snapper anglers fish on the bottom, and employ a basic Running Sinker rig. Variations include a small sinker that's allowed to run down to the bait, or a heavier sinker, which is stopped by a swivel about a metre along the line above the bait. When the snapper are hot, you can catch them not far from the surface on unweighted baits fed down a berley trail. In the same mood, snapper will take bait set under a bobby cork.

Some days you have to work different systems to get results. Sometimes simple variations on accepted methods are all that is needed to produce results.

Light Float rig

This rig is standard fare for anglers chasing top water pinfish including luderick, mullet, herring and garfish. The rig is best used in conjunction with a fine mist berley, which is dispersed and floats to bring the fish to the bait. In the case of luderick, lettuce weed mixed with sand does well. Split shot on the line is important. The shot acts to keep the bait down and add enough weight to ensure the float maintains the correct attitude.

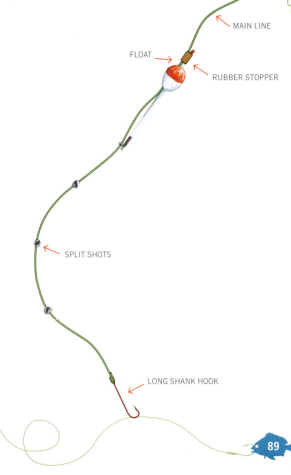

MAIN LINE

FLOAT

RUBBER STOPPER

SPLIT SHOTS

LONG SHANK HOOK

Paternoster rig (with single hook droppers)

A fishing favourite that is in common use in fresh and salt water, the Paternoster is used for a variety of species including snapper, pearl perch, salmon, redfin and yellowbelly. Sinker weight should suit conditions, and hook sizes are governed by bait size. When constructing this rig, be careful the leaders don't become tangled. The distance between leaders should be the equivalent of 2 leaders. So, if each leader is 20cm long, set them up at least 60cm apart. If you tie a snap swivel to the end of the main line you will be able to make quick sinker changes to suit changing conditions, such as tidal flow.

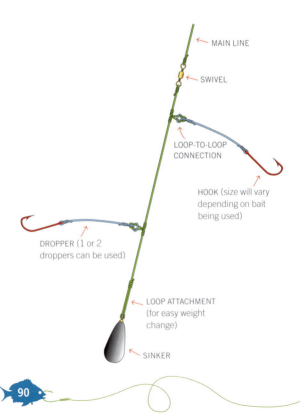

MAIN LINE

SWIVEL

LOOP-TO-LOOP
CONNECTION

HOOK (size will vary
depending on bait
being used)

DROPPER (1 or 2
droppers can be used)

LOOP ATTACHMENT
(for easy weight
change)

SINKER

The basic Running Sinker rig has a wide range of applications. In estuaries it can be used to catch flathead and bream, in rivers it is popular for yellowbelly, and bay anglers employ the rig to catch snapper. Any fish that feeds on the bottom is a possibility for this rig.

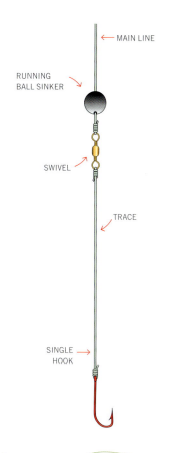

← MAIN LINE

RUNNING
BALL SINKER

SWIVEL

TRACE

SINGLE →
HOOK

Unweighted rig

RIGS ● General rigs

A good example of the KISS (Keep It Simple Stupid) concept, the basic hook on a line with no additional terminal tackle is an efficient rig. This system doesn't work in all waters. You can fish unweighted bait in current, but you must cast up current and allow time for it to sink. The effectiveness of this method depends on the weight and buoyancy of the bait used relative to water flow.

When light bait is used in strong current it will be swept out of the feeding lane and you will have to repeat the process. Some bait though, like whole prawns, work well in current as the lack of buoyancy allows the prawn to sink or hold depth. In any situation where unweighted bait can be used, it should be, as it is the most productive method to fish bait.

The hook is attached directly to your main line. The size of the hook will vary depending on target species and bait being used.

MAIN LINE

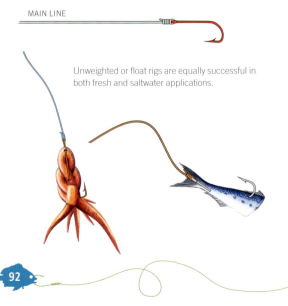

Unweighted or float rigs are equally successful in both fresh and saltwater applications.

Weighted rig (Running Sinker)

Bay, estuary, river and lake anglers all make use of this simple rig when seeking bottom feeders, or lowering a bait over the side of a boat and raising it off the bottom. When used to offer bait on the bottom, the rig is designed to allow a fish to take bait, and pull line through the sinker without feeling weight. For anglers bobbing baits, say a bunch of worms or shrimp for redfin or yellowbelly, the function of the sinker is to keep the bait below the surface. Although the sinker falls to the hook, this does not deter fish. An advantage of this rig is that longer, more accurate casts can be made due to the sinker being at the end of the line, rather than a metre or so above the bait and separated by a swivel that can cause the leader to swing and destabilize the cast.

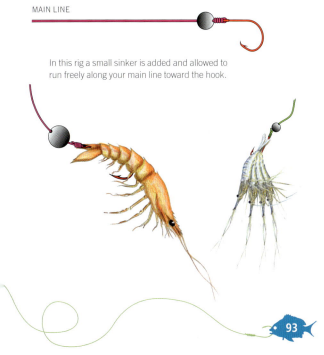

MAIN LINE

In this rig a small sinker is added and allowed to run freely along your main line toward the hook.

Balloon Live Bait rig

The average leader length from hook to double is about 3m, and should be a minimum 80kg breaking strain. When connecting the double to the leader, use a ball-bearing game swivel.

The most popular set-up is the 'Balloon rig', and it is easy to construct. A semi-inflated balloon, approximately 15cm diameter, is attached to the leader by a single strand of cotton or A-size binding thread. If you want your bait to swim deeper than your leader length, thread a swivel or Ezi-rig running sinker clip, minus the clip, to 1 strand of your double line, then tie the double to the swivel. A Stopper knot is tied onto the double to control the depth.

Keep the length of cotton to the balloon as short as possible, and never attach it directly to the line, always tie it to the swivel or whatever clip device you are working. When a tuna hits the bait it will feel little resistance because the cotton breaks easily.

Balloon size is governed by conditions. Given a strong tail wind you can increase balloon size to take advantage of the elements. Helium works well when the breeze is offshore. When fishing into an onshore wind keep the balloon size down to the size of a tennis ball, or less; the smaller profile reduces wind resistance.

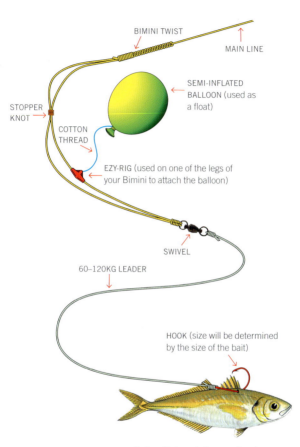

BIMINI TWIST

MAIN LINE

SEMI-INFLATED
BALLOON (used as
a float)

STOPPER
KNOT

COTTON
THREAD

EZY-RIG (used on one of the legs of
your Bimini to attach the balloon)

SWIVEL

60–120KG LEADER

HOOK (size will be determined
by the size of the bait)

Both yakka's and slimy mackerel
make excellent live bait.

Balloon Simple rig

This is a simpler version of the Balloon rig
whereby instead of attaching the balloon with thread,
the flared mouthpiece section of the balloon is pushed
through one of the eyes of the swivel. Water pressure
is enough to release the balloon, just make sure not
to push the actual knot from the balloon through the
swivel as it may lock and not release when taken.

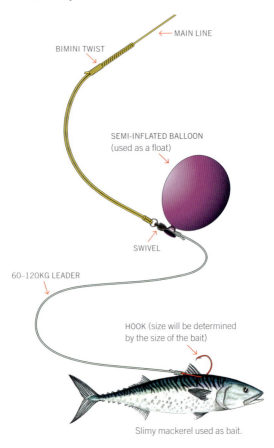

MAIN LINE

BIMINI TWIST

SEMI-INFLATED BALLOON
(used as a float)

SWIVEL

60–120KG LEADER

HOOK (size will be determined
by the size of the bait)

Slimy mackerel used as bait.

Blackfish (luderick) are finicky feeders, and setting the float correctly is about trial and error, with the weight governed by conditions and float size. Float attitude in the water is all important: the rig requires enough weight to sink the float and hold it in the vertical position, while pulling enough of the float under the surface so that minimal effort is required by the fish to pull it completely under. At the same time, a small amount of indicator must remain above water to indicate a bite.

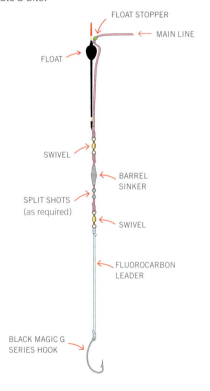

FLOAT STOPPER

← MAIN LINE

FLOAT →

SWIVEL →

→ BARREL SINKER

SPLIT SHOTS → (as required)

→ SWIVEL

← FLUOROCARBON LEADER

BLACK MAGIC G SERIES HOOK →

Float with Baited Squid Jig

This is a simple method to catch squid, one that takes the guesswork out of getting a hook-up as the squid does it for you. Equipment required is a polystyrene float, a bait jig spike and a fish such as whiting, mullet or yakka to thread on the jig.

A bait jig consists of a steel or aluminium shaft, about 4mm in diameter and about 20cm long. At one end of the shaft, a circle of pins pointing back towards the top is attached. The shaft is tapered at the top and has a hole drilled so the angler can attach the line via a clip swivel. To rig these jigs up you insert the shaft through the fish, which is tied to the shaft in some way to prevent squid from tearing it off; fuse wire does the job. Ensure the gill covers are wired shut to increase the longevity of your bait.

A bait jig under a float works when drifting over weed beds, from rock ledges and piers. An alternative method is to employ an artificial jig suspended beneath a 'Dink' float, which is a simple foam (polyethylene) tube about 14mm in diameter and 10–15cm long. Dink floats are light; super sensitive and buoyant to the point where any water motion causes them to move and this action is transferred down the line to the jig. The Dink float system is best used from a drifting boat in water less than 3m deep.

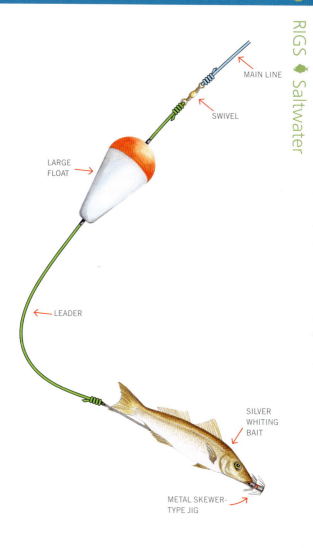

MAIN LINE

SWIVEL

LARGE
FLOAT

LEADER

SILVER
WHITING
BAIT

METAL SKEWER-
TYPE JIG

A connection employed when connecting a braid main line to a monofilament leader. A double is tied in the main line, which in turn is connected to the mono leader using either a Ducknose or Albright knot. The monofilament leader, which in light lines would be fluorocarbon, is a more abrasive resistant than braid, and adds some stretch to reduce the chance of a hook tearing free under load.

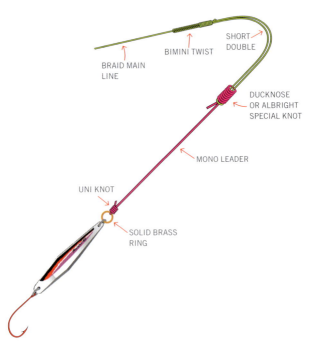

SHORT DOUBLE

BIMINI TWIST

BRAID MAIN LINE

DUCKNOSE OR ALBRIGHT SPECIAL KNOT

MONO LEADER

UNI KNOT

SOLID BRASS RING

Mulloway Running Sinker rig

Anglers chasing mulloway in Victorian estuaries employ this rig. The Double Nail knot acts as a Stopper for the sinker or Ezi-rig. As a result, the bait can swim (or float if dead) off the bottom and be away from pickers. The Slim Beauty knot, used to connect the leader to the Double Nail knot, could also be a Cats Paw if a wind-on leader is used, or an Albright in the case of a single strand of monofilament.

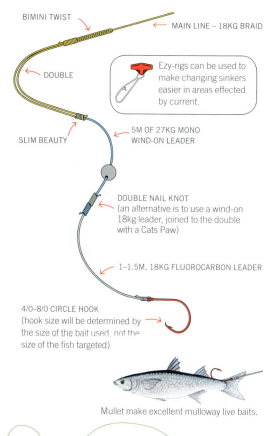

BIMINI TWIST

MAIN LINE – 18KG BRAID

DOUBLE

Ezy-rigs can be used to make changing sinkers easier in areas effected by current.

SLIM BEAUTY

5M OF 27KG MONO WIND-ON LEADER

DOUBLE NAIL KNOT (an alternative is to use a wind-on 18kg leader, joined to the double with a Cats Paw)

1–1.5M, 18KG FLUOROCARBON LEADER

4/0–8/0 CIRCLE HOOK (hook size will be determined by the size of the bait used, not the size of the fish targeted)

Mullet make excellent mulloway live baits.

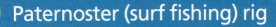

Paternoster (surf fishing) rig

Paternoster is Latin for the first words of the
Lord's Prayer: Our Father. This rig has nothing to do
with religion, although some anglers may be inclined
to call for help from above at times. In this diagram,
the Paternoster rig is set up for fishing for Australian
salmon, using a surf popper or soft plastic as an
attractor, attached to a snood above the bait. Snood
length and placement on main line should be such
that the snoods do not often tangle during casting.

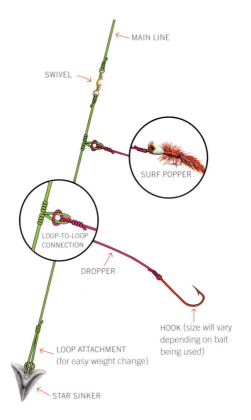

MAIN LINE

SWIVEL

SURF POPPER

LOOP-TO-LOOP
CONNECTION

DROPPER

HOOK (size will vary
depending on bait
being used)

LOOP ATTACHMENT
(for easy weight change)

STAR SINKER

When you want to fish in current or surf areas
where you are seeking big fish, this is the rig to employ.
It is popular with surf fishers chasing mulloway and
gummy sharks, and with anglers fishing for snapper in
areas where current is a major influence.

A Running Paternoster is designed to hold a bait off
the seabed in the same way a Fixed Paternoster rig
does, however the major difference is that when a
fish takes the bait you can feed line out so there is
no resistance.

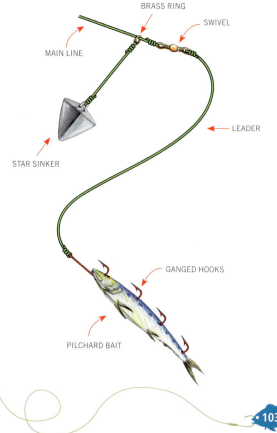

BRASS RING

SWIVEL

MAIN LINE

STAR SINKER

LEADER

GANGED HOOKS

PILCHARD BAIT

PVA Mesh

PVA Mesh is a dissolvable material used to
disperse berley alongside bait when fishing for carp
in Europe. Variations on the theme can be used for
bottom species including snapper. A PVA bag full of
berley is attached to one of the bait hooks and cast
out. PVA bags are a soluble netting material that
dissolves in water in about 30 seconds leaving the
bait surrounded by the berley. It's a neat idea. Some
anglers soak their PVA bags in water before casting so
that these dissolve as the bait is sinking.

1. Start by removing the plunger
from the cylinder, and work
some of the mesh material
toward the bottom of the tube.

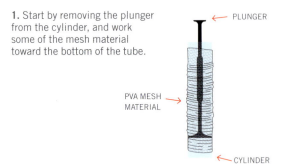

PLUNGER

PVA MESH
MATERIAL

CYLINDER

2. Tie a knot in the end of the mesh material, allowing it to
hang off the bottom of the tube. Remove the plunger and
start adding fish scraps or any other items you wish to berley
with. Use the plunger to press and compact your berley.

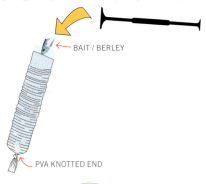

BAIT / BERLEY

PVA KNOTTED END

3. You can make your PVA berley bag as large or as small as you like. Approximately 5–7cm is fine for saltwater applications.

4. Once you have reached the desired size, pull a little more mesh off the bottom of the cylinder. Make sure you leave enough length so that you can tie another knot on top to seal the bag.

5. Attach the PVA bag to one of the hooks running through your bait. As your bait sinks and comes in contact with water, the PVA mesh material will start to shrink and form a tighter and more plump shape. After approximately 30 seconds, the PVA material will begin to dissolve and breakdown. As this occurs your berley is released in and around the location of your bait.

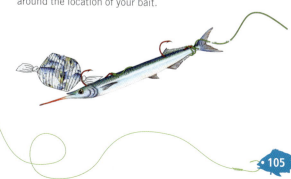

Two-Hook rig, Fixed

This standard running sinker rig is the most popular rig employed to catch bottom feeders like snapper, bream, whiting, flathead and gummy sharks. It is most effective in bay and estuary waters.

The idea behind this rig is that it gives an angler the ability to allow a fish to take bait without feeling any resistance. When all goes according to plan, line runs free through the sinker as the fish moves away with the bait, the angler waits, engages the reel and sets the hook.

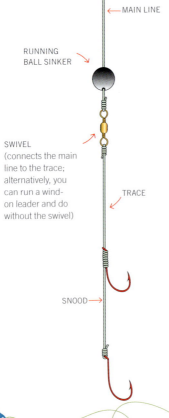

← MAIN LINE

RUNNING
BALL SINKER

SWIVEL
(connects the main
line to the trace;
alternatively, you
can run a wind-
on leader and do
without the swivel)

TRACE

SNOOD →

Two-Hook Slider rig, Snapper

The Snapper Two-Hook slider rig is traditionally the most common double hook set up where the second or sliding hook acts as a keeper. The rig can be put together in various ways. Thread a sinker on the main line, attach a swivel to act as a stopper, and then add about 1m of leader material (15kg minimum) to the bottom eye of the swivel. The swivel reduces line twist. A disadvantage of this rig is that because the second hook is not fixed it is less likely to hook a snapper. This is not a common occurrence but for consistency the Fixed Two-Hook rig is preferred.

RIGS ◆ Saltwater

Both fresh garfish and silver whiting make excellent snapper baits.

← MAIN LINE

RUNNING
BALL SINKER

SWIVEL
(connects
your main line
to your trace)

TRACE

SECOND HOOK
(allowed to
slide freely)

Whiting Nipper rig

Standard running sinker with a size 16 keeper hook, which is allowed to slide on the leader. This rig is used when fishing with nippers for sand whiting along the east coast. The keeper hook goes through the tail with the bait-holding hook through the side of the body of the nipper.

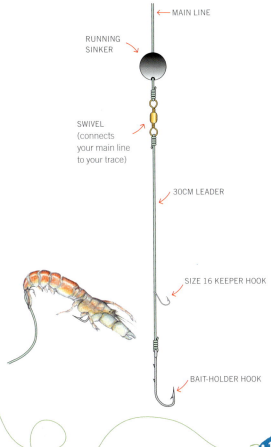

← MAIN LINE

RUNNING
SINKER

SWIVEL
(connects
your main line
to your trace)

30CM LEADER

SIZE 16 KEEPER HOOK

BAIT-HOLDER HOOK

Whiting Running Sinker

In the south, anglers fishing for King George whiting prefer a lighter version of a Running Paternoster when fishing strong current, with a leader about 2m long. In bay or estuary situations, where current is minimal, the standard Running Sinker rig shown here is popular. The red plastic tubing or red beads act as an attractor for the fish.

← MAIN LINE

RUNNING
SINKER

SWIVEL
(connects
your main line
to your trace)

30CM LEADER

RED PLASTIC
TUBE OR BEADS

LONG SHANK
HOOK

This system employs a Dacron loop to connect a double line to a single monofilament leader. It was developed so that the angler can manage fish closer to the boat by allowing the leader to pass through the rod guides, and bring fish closer for tracing.

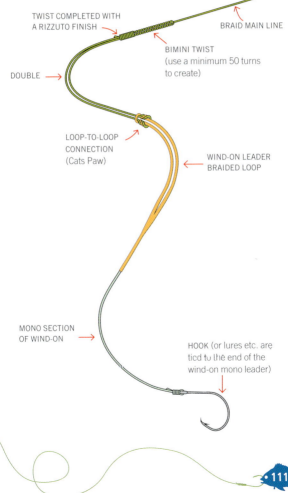

TWIST COMPLETED WITH A RIZZUTO FINISH

BRAID MAIN LINE

BIMINI TWIST
(use a minimum 50 turns to create)

DOUBLE

LOOP-TO-LOOP
CONNECTION
(Cats Paw)

WIND-ON LEADER
BRAIDED LOOP

MONO SECTION
OF WIND-ON

HOOK (or lures etc. are tied to the end of the wind-on mono leader)

Wire Float rig

The Wire Float rig is a jetty favourite but is also useful when fishing from rock walls, and even from a boat. Some pelagic species, like barracouta and mackerel need wire trace. This rig is also useful if you want to hook small sharks or tailor. The swivel acts as a stopper, and split shot on the line is desirable to keep the float at the correct attitude and to ensure the bait is kept at the required depth.

MAIN LINE

SWIVEL

FLOAT

SPLIT SHOTS

SWIVEL

WIRE TRACE

PILCHARD BAIT

Bubble Float and Mudeye rig

A simple method used from a boat or shore, for trout in lakes whereby a mudeye, minnow or glassie is suspended under the bubble float. These floats have a tube that passes through the centre and acts as a pump to fill the bubble with the required amount of water; the more water, the heavier the float and the further the angler can cast. Placing a small piece of cork or stopper on the line above the float controls bait depth. To enable casting, the distance from the stopper to the hook should be no more than the rod length. This rig is also used in estuary environments by anglers bait fishing for the bass look-alike, estuary perch. In this case the bait used is a cricket.

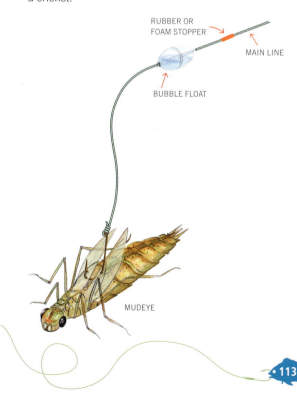

RUBBER OR FOAM STOPPER

MAIN LINE

BUBBLE FLOAT

MUDEYE

Crappie rig

The Crappie rig is commonplace in North American lakes, in this case Mark Twain Lake on the Salt River, Missouri. Anglers use the rig to fish for a tasty redfin look-alike, the crappie – pronounced croppy. It is a double Paternoster, the main difference being that the bottom hook is below the sinker as you would for King George whiting. DuWaynne Azotec, a Missouri fishing guide, showed the rig off. He tied on no. 2 long shank hooks that he had coloured, orange or yellow, using powder coating he bought from the tackle shop.

DuWaynne said the colouring on the hooks was an added attractor for the crappie. The hook is placed through the jaws of the baitfish, which are then lowered to the rocky bottom. He fished it about 10m from shore and drifted along the edge, allowing the rig to bounce off rocks, hoping it would not become snagged.

Fish caught on this rig in Australia include redfin and yellowbelly in fresh water, and flathead in salt water.

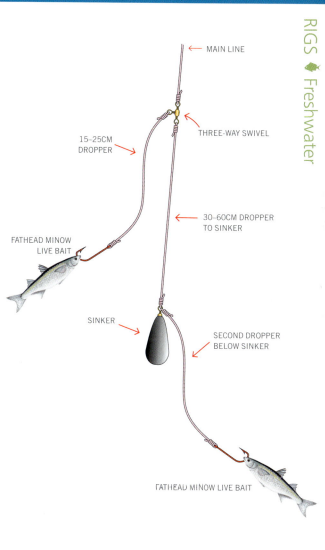

MAIN LINE

THREE-WAY SWIVEL

15–25CM DROPPER

30–60CM DROPPER TO SINKER

FATHEAD MINOW LIVE BAIT

SINKER

SECOND DROPPER BELOW SINKER

FATHEAD MINOW LIVE BAIT

Downrigging

Downrigging is a popular technique used in lakes when trolling lures for trout. This system is preferred among serious anglers to the older method of tying in a plastic paravane on the line.

DOWNRIGGER

LINE BELLIE

DOWNRIGGER WIRE

LEAD BOMB

RELEASE CLIP

The downrigger has a lead weight, called a bomb, attached to a wire cable, which in turn is lowered to a desired depth. The line to the lure is attached to the bomb via a release clip. Downrigger clips must have tension adjustment and be strong to hold the lure used. Rods need to be loaded because you cannot allow loose line to trail between rod tip and bomb as there will be slack in the water, and when a fish hits you may miss the strike.

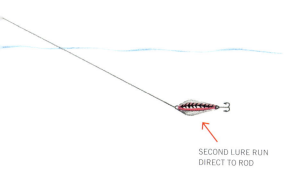

SECOND LURE RUN
DIRECT TO ROD

DROP BACK
TO LURE

Hair rig

European anglers use this rig to catch carp.

Gary Allen, a guide at Mequinenza, Spain, introduced us to this rig. His Hair rig consisted of a no. 8 hook tied to the leader, then it had a loop of braid running off the back of the hook. This loop is threaded through a bait called a boilie and held in place by a plastic stopper. Boilies are spherical balls of bait made from 'secret ingredients' that are mixed together, boiled and then moulded.

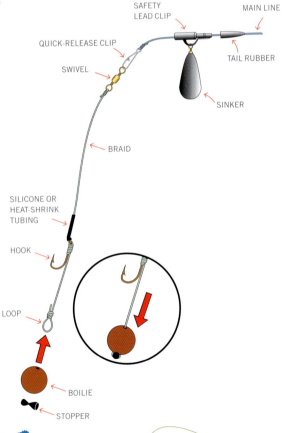

SAFETY LEAD CLIP

MAIN LINE

QUICK-RELEASE CLIP

TAIL RUBBER

SWIVEL

SINKER

BRAID

SILICONE OR HEAT-SHRINK TUBING

HOOK

LOOP

BOILIE

STOPPER

Pencil Float

The Pencil Float can be employed to fish for
most pelagic species in river, lakes, bays and
estuaries. The differences between the fish you catch
are bait and hook sizes. A few examples are:

- lake – trout – no.14 hook and a mudeye
- bay – garfish – no. 8–10 hook and pipi
- estuary – mullet – no. 6 hook and sandworm
- river – redfin – no. 6 hook and scrubworm.

There are many variations and many more species
that will rise in a water column to feed just under the
surface. The depth setting from float to bait is judged
on the feeding area of the fish, be it shallow weed
bed or deep water around pier pilings. Floats are not
designed to lie flat on the surface but to be vertical.
The split shot is important to keep the bait down and
should be heavy enough to sink the float up to the
indicator colour at the top.

MAIN LINE

SLEEVE FOR FLOAT
DEPTH ADJUSTMENT

PENCIL FLOAT

SPLIT SHOTS

Sturgeon rig

On the Fraser River in British Columbia, Canada, white sturgeon is much sought after. White sturgeon is a creature with prehistoric links dating back 175 million years, and one of the largest freshwater fishes in the world. The bait is started with a 57mm square of fine mesh, such as pantyhose material. When the square is cut, a tablespoon of orange salmon eggs is placed on the material, which is folded over the eggs and twisted at the top. A hosiery string is tied around the twist to keep the package together. When finished, an 8/0 hook is inserted to complete the sturgeon bait. The rig is a Running Sinker and is similar to Running Paternoster rigs used in Australia for snapper and mulloway.

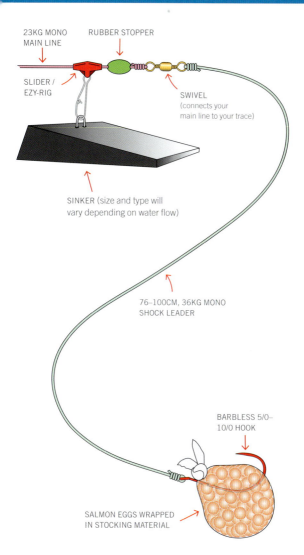

23KG MONO
MAIN LINE

RUBBER STOPPER

SLIDER /
EZY-RIG

SWIVEL
(connects your
main line to your trace)

SINKER (size and type will
vary depending on water flow)

76–100CM, 36KG MONO
SHOCK LEADER

BARBLESS 5/0–
10/0 HOOK

SALMON EGGS WRAPPED
IN STOCKING MATERIAL

Wels Catfish

Gary Allen, a fishing guide in Spain, uses this rig on the Segre and Ebro rivers at Mequinenza when fishing for Wels Catfish. The catfish grow to more than 50kg and Gary said when the river was low, you could see the reeds moving as catfish hunted among them. 'It's all about stopping power,' Gary said. 'We need to stop the catfish running into the reeds, and if it does get there then the heavy leader won't rub away on the reeds.'

For leader there are a couple of metres of 2mm diameter roller blind cord. The hook is a 6/0 O'Shaunnesy straight shank and the rig is similar to the Hair rig used for carp in that a pellet is suspended below the hook.

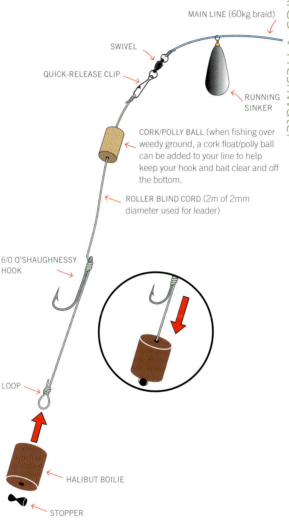

MAIN LINE (60kg braid)

SWIVEL

QUICK-RELEASE CLIP

RUNNING SINKER

CORK/POLLY BALL (when fishing over weedy ground, a cork float/polly ball can be added to your line to help keep your hook and bait clear and off the bottom.

ROLLER BLIND CORD (2m of 2mm diameter used for leader)

6/0 O'SHAUGHNESSY HOOK

LOOP

HALIBUT BOILIE

STOPPER

Belly Teaser

RIGS ● Game and offshore

The Belly Teaser rig is used to enhance a trolled skirted lure and is effective on sailfish and marlin, fish that often rise to bait or lure to check it out before striking. The additional smell adds to the bubble trail caused by the lure and this can be catalyst for a strike.

1. Using mack tuna, striped tuna, mackerel or dolphin fish, cut out the belly section of the fish including the ventral fin area.

AREA TO BE CUT OUT

2. Make a small cut down part of the mid-line so that the flap folds in half.

TRIM TO SHAPE

3. Remove the hooks from a skirted lure. Fold the flap in half and prepare to sew the flap with heavy, waxed thread and a bait needle.

OPEN LOOP

CRIMP

4. Fold the belly strip in half and using heavy, waxed thread sew the front end together over the leader. Make sure that the front of the belly strip is tight and secure. On completion make sure the skirt goes right over the belly strip.

Bridle rig for slow-trolled live bait

Bridle rigging live fish is the preferred method for slow trolling. Ideally, the fish should be unharmed by the experience of being rigged. If you don't like the concept of passing a needle through the top of the eye sockets there is also a fleshy area on the nose of most fish that can be used to the same purpose. In practice, one end of the bridle lead is attached to the hook, the baitfish is held in a wet towel and then the needle and line inserted, and the line tied off on the hook. The process should take less than a minute and it takes 2 pairs of hands to make the rigging up smooth.

1. First, take a 30cm piece of 23kg braid, fold it in half and then double overhand knot it every 1.5–2cm.

KNOTTED BRAID

2. Attach the knotted braid to the hook by passing it around the hook and looping it through itself. Then attach your bait needle to the last loop furthest away from the hook.

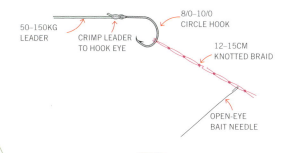

50–150KG LEADER

CRIMP LEADER TO HOOK EYE

8/0–10/0 CIRCLE HOOK

12–15CM KNOTTED BRAID

OPEN-EYE BAIT NEEDLE

3. Pass the bait needle through the top of the eye socket, staying above the eye. Pull the braid loop completely through and out the other side. This technique can be used on baits like slimy mackerel, yakkas, bonito and small tuna.

4. Loop and secure the end braid loop back twice around the hook. Make sure that the hook is left well clear of the bait's head (4cm minimum).

APPROXIMATELY 4–6CM LENGTH

Constructed from a single strand of monofilament,
the shark fly leader is designed to turn a large fly over
and is best manufactured with 8–15kg monofilament.
Owing to the manner of tying, the leader has an inbuilt
elasticity under load. The first stage is to tie a double
knot and then roll the 2 strands together to create a
Twisted Leader (Bungie) knot. This length of Twisted
Leader is halved by folding back on itself, and rolled
together again to give 4 strands, which in turn become
a heavy butt section. Use a Nail knot to lock it off,
which eliminates a knot from the leader. The knot
works in one thirds so that the butt section is a third,
the double Twisted Leader about one third and this
then runs into the single-strand leader to which is tied
a piano wire joined to the tippet with an Albright knot.
All up, the leader should not be longer than 2m.

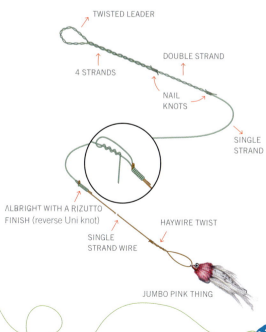

TWISTED LEADER

4 STRANDS

DOUBLE STRAND

NAIL KNOTS

SINGLE STRAND

ALBRIGHT WITH A RIZUTTO FINISH (reverse Uni knot)

SINGLE STRAND WIRE

HAYWIRE TWIST

JUMBO PINK THING

Skipping Gar

Simple to create, yet oh so effective on surface species, the Skipping Gar relies on the combination of sight and smell to attract high-speed predators like marlin, sailfish, tuna, yellowtail kingfish and mackerel. This rig is often the most effective option for yellowfin tuna when the golden sickles are feeding on that garfish look-alike, the saury. The size of the skirt used to cover the head of the bait is governed by the garfish. Avoid expensive skirts as the quality of plastic or brand name have no bearing on the effectiveness of this rig. The copper wire can be replaced with pre-made wire spirals available from most tackle stores.

1. 50–70KG LEADER

10/0 S12S GAMAKATSU
SALTWATER FLY HOOK

7–10CM PINK SQUID
SKIRT OR SIMILAR

CRIMP

12CM
COPPER
WIRE OR
SIMILAR

2. Measure the hook against the gar, so that the eye of the hook sits level with the eye of the gar – work out the hook exit point.

CUT OFF THE BILL WITH
SCISSORS OR A SHARP KNIFE

HOOK EXIT POINT

3. Pass the hook through the mouth of the gar, and bend the bait until the hook exits through the exit point.

4. Pass the copper wire through the head of the bait (centre) and bind around the mouth to keep it shut.

5. Slide the squid skirt down over the gar's head and fit snuggly.

Skirted Lure

Correct rigging of a large Skirted Lure for big gamefish such as marlin requires attention to detail. It is not enough to pass a line through the lure and tie on a hook; big lures are for big fish, and to run through the sea and hold the fish these lures need strength and balance. Close attention to detail is paramount. The system shown in the diagram is proven, so there is no need to deviate.

ARMOUR SPRING

180KG LEADER

2.3MM CRIMP

30CM SKIRTED LURE

BALLCOCK WASHER

CRIMP

STAINLESS SHACKLE

METAL THIMBLE

CRIMP

2MM STAINLESS WIRE

WAX TAPE

11/0 HOOKS SET AT 180° TO EACH OTHER

HEAT SHRINK

Trolling and rigging dead bait

How you rig the bait is determined by whether you want it to swim or to skip, and some baits suit some applications better than others. Slimy mackerel and yellowtail scad can be rigged either way, and the alternate rig from skip bait to swimmer can involve tying in a small sinker below the jaw. The yakka shown is rigged as swimming bait. To maintain the bait's upright attitude in the water, a small, round sinker is threaded on to the bridle to sit below the chin. Trolling baits are subjected to a lot of stress caused by pounding in the water, which can tear flesh away, making the bait useless; as water enters inside trolled bait, pressure can build, which in turn will cause the entrails to blow out. To prevent this, make a short slit in the belly of the bait and remove the stomach contents. Then reach in through the gills and remove the rakers (so you can close the gill plates more firmly), then sew shut the mouth, gill plates and belly slit to prevent as much water intrusion as possible.

Most charter boats brine or salt their baits, which firms the flesh and gives bait longer water-life.

The bridle of leader is formed to provide a centralised towing point that ensures an even pull and prevents the bait spinning. It is important to position this bridle dead centre. Pick a spot on the fish's head, midway between the eyes, and push the bait needle down and back through the head. Aim the needle back to exit at a point about 3–4mm behind the isthmus (this is the gristle part of the fish's throat, behind the gill slits, ahead of the pectoral fins).

When stitching up the mouth of the bait, locate the leader loop in the notch you have cut into the front of the top and bottom jaws. This ensures the thread doesn't slip away to one side and allow the mouth to open.

Always test the bait by dragging it alongside the boat so you can see how it behaves. If it doesn't swim perfectly, work on it until it does.

1. First select a hook size to match the size of the bait being used. Remove the eyes of the bait and measure the exit point of the hook so that the eye of the hook is positioned directly under the centre of the head.

2. Create a small cut and pass the hook up from the measured point.

3. Place an uncrimped crimp on your leader and using a bait needle, pass your leader directly through the centre of the head making sure the line passes through the eye of the hook.

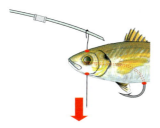

4. Take a suitable-sized bean sinker that fits flush up against the gill cavity, usually between 15–45g, depending on the bait size. Crimp the leader closed on a loose loop, always trying to keep things centred.

5. Finally, using a bait needle and waxed thread, sew the mouth and gills of the bait shut.

RIGS ● Game and offshore

Trolling spread

There are many spread variations for lures. The three shown here are:

- staggered – each lure is set at a different distance behind the boat
- parallel – a pair of lures is trailed behind the boat at the same distance to create a symmetrical pattern
- mixed grill – where different types of lures are combined through a lure spread; hard body and skirted lures can be trolled together, however troll speed must suit slowest lure.

When setting the lure distance, sit the lure to run on the face of the pressure wave behind the boat. This will maximise efficiency and strike rate.

Staggered lure spread

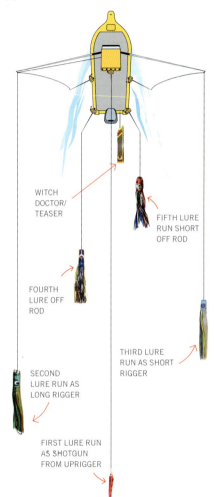

WITCH
DOCTOR/
TEASER

FIFTH LURE
RUN SHORT
OFF ROD

FOURTH
LURE OFF
ROD

THIRD LURE
RUN AS SHORT
RIGGER

SECOND
LURE RUN AS
LONG RIGGER

FIRST LURE RUN
AS SHOTGUN
FROM UPRIGGER

Parallel lure spread

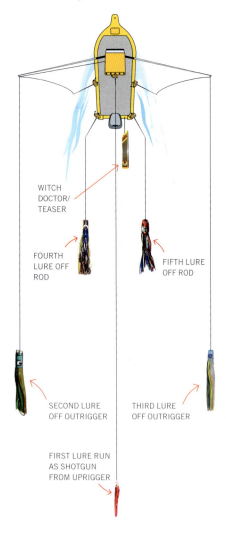

WITCH DOCTOR/ TEASER

FOURTH LURE OFF ROD

FIFTH LURE OFF ROD

SECOND LURE OFF OUTRIGGER

THIRD LURE OFF OUTRIGGER

FIRST LURE RUN AS SHOTGUN FROM UPRIGGER

Mixed grill lure spread

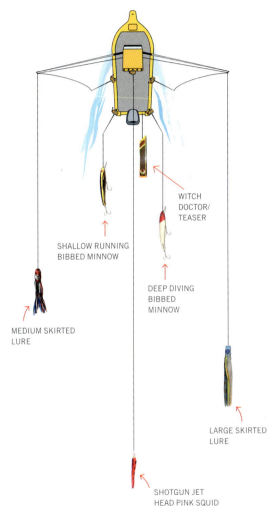

WITCH
DOCTOR/
TEASER

SHALLOW RUNNING
BIBBED MINNOW

DEEP DIVING
BIBBED
MINNOW

MEDIUM SKIRTED
LURE

LARGE SKIRTED
LURE

SHOTGUN JET
HEAD PINK SQUID

Carolina rig

Similar to Australia's standard Running Sinker rig, Carolina rigs were developed in the US in the 1970s by soft-plastic anglers. A Carolina rig separates the hook and lure from the lead with a leader. To tie one, you slip a lead on your line, follow it with a bead and then tie on a barrel swivel. A leader of varying length is tied to the swivel, and a hook tied to the leader. Hook size varies with the size of the lure used. Lead weight depends on conditions and can vary from 5–28g and leader length can be from a few centimetres to a couple of metres. Standard rigs consist of a 14g sinker and a 60cm leader. The rule of thumb is the clearer the water, the longer the leader; heavier lead is needed for the longer leaders and the deeper the water, the heavier the lead.

MAIN LINE

BULLET-SHAPED
RUNNING SINKER
(lead)

SWIVEL

LEADER

WEIGHTLESS HOOK

The Floater rig was developed for presenting unweighted, soft plastic lures, either on the surface or in shallow water where weed is a problem, hence the weedless hook. The hook is almost buried in the lure, with just the point protruding and running parallel along the back of the soft plastic.

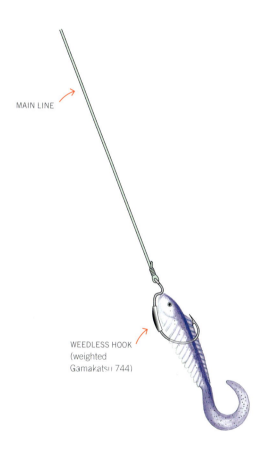

MAIN LINE

WEEDLESS HOOK
(weighted
Gamakatsu 744)

Texas rig

The Texas rig is a soft-plastic rig used to present lures on the bottom. The lure is unweighted for maximum action and the sinker employed is the lightest you can get away with allowing for wind when casting, and current during presentation. The rig is popular with worm-style, plastic lures. To be most effective use a weedless hook such as the Mustad Powerbite.

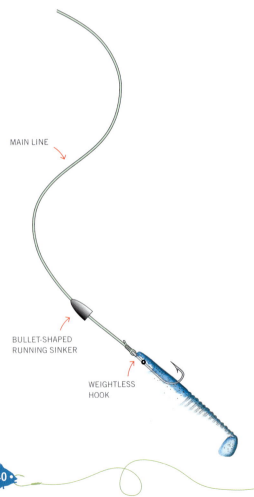

MAIN LINE

BULLET-SHAPED
RUNNING SINKER

WEIGHTLESS
HOOK

A variation on the multi-hook baitfish jig, the Twin Plastics rig suits bottom bouncing for smaller species such as flathead or pinkies. It does not suit medium to large fish. Due to its design it is best used for straight up-and-down jigging and is appropriate for working clear areas along reef systems.

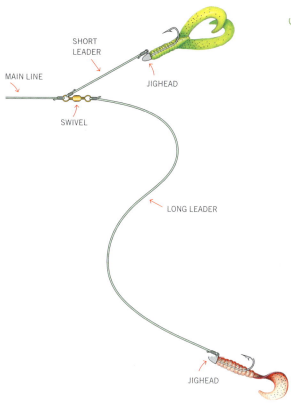

SHORT LEADER

MAIN LINE

JIGHEAD

SWIVEL

LONG LEADER

JIGHEAD

INDEX

142

Acknowledgements

The publisher would like to acknowledge the following individuals and organisations:

Commissioning editor
Melissa Krafchek

Project manager and editor
Alison Proietto

Design
Julie Thompson of
Penny Black Design

Layout
Megan Ellis

Index
Max McMaster

Pre-press
Splitting Image, Megan Ellis

Explore Australia Publishing
Pty Ltd
Ground Floor, Building 1,
658 Church Street,
Richmond, VIC 3121

Explore Australia Publishing Pty
Ltd is a division of Hardie Grant
Publishing Pty Ltd

hardie grant publishing

Published by Explore Australia
Publishing Pty Ltd, 2013

A Cataloguing-in-Publication entry
is available from the catalogue of
the National Library of Australia at
www.nla.gov.au

ISBN-13 9781741174212

10 9 8 7 6 5 4 3 2 1

Printed and bound in China by
1010 Printing International Ltd

Publisher's note: Every effort
has been made to ensure that
the information in this book is
accurate at the time of going to
press. The publisher welcomes
information and suggestions for
correction or improvement. Email:
info@exploreaustralia.net.au

Publisher's disclaimer: The
publisher cannot accept
responsibility for any errors or
omissions. The representation on
the maps of any road or track is
not necessarily evidence of public
right of way. The publisher cannot
be held responsible for any injury,
loss or damage incurred during
travel. It is vital to research any
proposed trip thoroughly and
seek the advice of relevant state
and travel organisations before
you leave.

www.exploreaustralia.net.au
Follow us on Twitter: @ExploreAus
Find us on Facebook: www.
  facebook.com/exploreaustralia